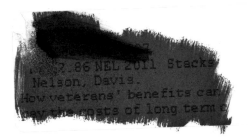
How Veterans' Benefits Can Pay the Costs of Long Term Care

Davis Nelson
Georgia VA Benefits and Medicaid Planning Attorney

DEDICATION

TO VETERANS AND THEIR FAMILIES —
THE BEST CLIENTS IN THE WORLD!

CONTENTS

ABOUT THE AUTHOR

 Davis Nelson has been representing veterans and their families since 1972. He limits his practice to VA benefits, Medicaid and estate planning.

If you have not already visited his web site at DavisNelsonLaw.com, please do so. It's got a ton of useful and valuable information, including the most up to date information about VA benefits and Georgia Medicaid. You can also visit Davis's blog at DavisNelson-Law.com/davis-blog.

Davis has been a lawyer for 39 years. He is a 1972 graduate with a Master of Laws degree from the advanced taxation program at the New York University Law School. He is an honors graduate of the University of Denver College of Law. He has represented individuals and businesses in tax, estate and business planning matters involving more than 40 countries.

Davis is VA-accredited, and is a member of ElderCounsel, WealthCounsel and the National Care Planning Council. Davis was an adjunct professor of taxation at Robert Morris University for 25 years. He is a member of the bar in Georgia, North Carolina, Pennsylvania, the District of Columbia, and Colorado.

Contact the Author:

Davis W. Nelson
Attorney and Counselor at Law
2002 Summit Blvd NE, Suite 300
Atlanta, Georgia 30319
Tel. 404.348.4263
Web site: davisnelsonlaw.com
Email: davis@davisnelsonlaw.com

DAN'S STORY

A society can be judged, in part, by how it treats its military veterans — how it cares for those who, in the words of Abraham Lincoln, "have borne the battle."

The United States offers a confusing array of financial and nonfinancial support to its veterans, reflecting the grateful, caring nature of the American people. Through the U.S. Department of Veterans Affairs (the VA), veterans, their dependents, and their survivors can apply for a broad range of programs and services that can make their lives better.

Eligibility for most of these veterans benefits require that the veteran's discharge from active duty military service be classified as better than dishonorable. Note that I did not say that the veteran's discharge must be honorable — only that it be other than dishonorable.

Active service ordinarily requires some full-time service, other than your periods of active duty training, as a member of one of the military branches or certain other government agencies such as the Public Health Service.

Many of the programs are need-based; that is, there are financial requirements for eligibility, in addition to the nonfinancial qualifications. If a veteran does not meet the financial qualifications today, often the veteran can take steps to become financially eligible, with the assistance of a financial professional.

There are two programs in particular that are of interest to veterans and their families who are struggling with the sometimes devastating costs of long term care, either for the veteran or a member of the veteran's family. They are the focus of this book. In the pages that follow, one is called Compensation and the other is called Pension, though they are more commonly known by other names.

There was a time when both of these programs were unknown to me, just at the time when my family most needed them. There are hundreds of thousands of Georgia veterans and their family members who should know about the programs but don't. They are as unaware as I once was. That's why I wrote this book. As a colleague of mine likes to say, "If we don't help these veterans and their families, then who will?"

If only I had known what I know now, my life and the lives of my father-in-law Dan and his family would have been very different.

Dan was born and lived most of his life in Pittsburgh, Pennsylvania. His formal education ended after high school. Like countless other boys, his ambition was to get a job in one of the many steel mills that lined both banks of the Monongahela River that joins the Allegheny in downtown Pittsburgh to form the Ohio River.

At the time, steelworkers' wages were the highest of any blue collar job in the world. So, when Dan finally got his dream job, he was assigned to a mill in the small local community of McKees Rocks making railroad car axles, a hot, dirty, dangerous job.

A few months later, the United States entered World War Two in December 1941.

Dan continued to work in the steel mill until 1943. That year, he got married, but the newlyweds' only honeymoon was a train trip to Baltimore where Dan reported for duty with the Navy.

From 1943 until early 1946, Dan served as a radioman on the seaplane tender *USS Currituck* in the Pacific.

After the war, Dan returned to the steel mill, where he worked until he was stricken with stomach cancer in the 1970s. Since he wasn't able to work any longer, he retired early on a very small pension and social security. From that time on, Dan was never again able to work and his family struggled financially.

Dan had many close brushes with death from his cancer, once being told he would not live out the week. But miraculously, Dan recovered and lived on until his death at age 84.

Throughout his later years, he had to be institutionalized a half dozen times, often for months or years at a time. You can imagine the incredible financial burden all this was on his family.

After I married his daughter, I offered to try to find ways to supplement Dan's income, but frankly I wasn't very successful. Even though I was a lawyer, it never occurred to me to approach the VA for help. Even if I had, it is unlikely I would have uncovered or appreciated the long term care benefit commonly known as "aid and attendance."

After Dan's death, his widow was left with little more than a small monthly social security check. It was only years later that I discovered how the VA can be there for veterans like Dan and surviving spouses like Dan's widow.

Only years later did I come to understand how the little-known benefits described in this book can dramatically improve the lives of veteran households. These VA benefits just might do the same for you.

Now, for veterans like Dan and for surviving spouses like Dan's widow, I can secure a VA Pension of hundreds, even thousands, of dollars each and every month for the rest of their lives. I will spread the good news. And I will not let another veteran lose out on what they earned and deserve.

If I don't help, then who will?

I
INTRODUCTION TO VA PENSION AND COMPENSATION

There are more than 765,000 veterans here in the State of Georgia. There may be half again as many surviving spouses and other dependents of deceased veterans. That would bring the total number of veterans and deceased veterans' family members to more than one million.

It's estimated several hundred thousand of these Georgia veterans and family members are eligible to receive VA cash benefits, yet perhaps no more than 50,000 are actually receiving those benefits.

Why is the number so low?

There are many reasons why, some of which I discuss in the pages that follow. But first you need to know more about those benefits and what they can do for you.

TWO VA DISABILITY PROGRAMS

VA administers two important disability benefit programs. One we will refer to as *Compensation*. The other we will call *Pension*. You may have heard the latter program referred to as "aid and attendance." One thing you will learn is why the label "aid and attendance" is an inadequate description of this valuable benefit.

One other thing you should note at the outset is that, when we use the term "disability," we are including long term care. For the most part, a need for long term care by a veteran or family member is deemed a disability.

When a person requires the assistance of someone else to help with his or her physical or emotional needs over an extended period of time, this is known as long term care. Such help may be required for many of the activities or needs that those of us who are healthy and active take for granted.

The needed assistance may include such activities as walking, bathing, dressing, doing laundry, and shopping. The need may be due to many causes such as disability, illness, injury, the infirmity of old age, or a terminal condition. Most of us will need help of this kind at some point in our lives.

The need for long term care may be for only a few weeks or months, or it could last for many years. A temporary need for care may arise due to a stay in a rehabilitation facility or during a period of recovery from illness or injury.

Chronic conditions may require longer term care. This type of care is becoming more common because of the increasing incidence of dementia and other factors that affect our mental faculties, often brought on by the fact we're living longer than in earlier times.

Such care may be needed in many different settings, depending on the wishes of the family and the person in need of the care. In my experience, those needing care prefer to live in the following settings, in the order listed:

- IN THE RECIPIENT'S HOME
- IN THE HOME OF A FAMILY MEMBER OR FRIEND
- AT AN ADULT DAY CARE FACILITY
- ASSISTED LIVING FACILITY
- HOSPICE
- NURSING HOME

DISABILITY COMPENSATION

The first disability income benefit is called *Compensation*. It is intended to provide the veteran a certain amount of monthly income to compensate for the potential loss of lifetime income in the private sector due to a disability, injury or illness incurred during the veteran's military service.

In order to receive Compensation, the veteran must provide evidence of a service-connected disability. Most veterans who are receiving this benefit were awarded an amount based on a percentage of disability shortly after they left the active service. There is generally no income or asset qualification for most forms of Compensation and the benefit is nontaxable.

There is a surviving spouse death benefit associated with Compensation, based on the same principles.

In my experience, there may be a large number of Georgia veterans having service-connected disabilities but who never applied for the benefit, for a variety of reasons. If you think you may fall into this group, you may not be too late. VA may accept your late application. This may pay off in multiple ways — not just in the cash Compensation, but could also earn you other long term VA care services as well.

Some veterans may have a record of being exposed to extreme cold, having an in-service, non-disabling injury, having tropical diseases or tuberculosis or other incidents or exposures that at the time may not have shown signs of any disability but years later have resulted in medical problems. Most elderly veterans who never applied for Compensation may not realize they can apply many years after leaving the service. In fact, VA has acknowledged this problem and in 2006 conducted an outreach program to these veterans in five states with low elderly Compensation enrollment and ended up adding an additional 8,000 beneficiaries to the rolls!

One of the more common situations I see in my office is a veteran who is receiving Compensation but whose condition has worsened over the years. They can reapply and get a larger amount based on a higher disability rating, with appropriate medical proof.

PENSION

Pension is the second of the two disability income benefit programs from VA. The purpose of this benefit is to provide supplemental income to disabled or older veterans who have a low income, or high income and high long term care costs. Pension is for wartime veterans who have disabilities (long term care needs) which are not connected to their active-duty service.

If a veteran's income exceeds the Pension amount, then there will be no award. However, income can be adjusted downward for out-of-pocket medical expenses, and this allows veterans with household incomes larger than the Pension amount to qualify for a monthly benefit. There is also an asset test to qualify for Pension.

"Aid and attendance" is the commonly used term for this little-known veterans' disability income program. The reason for using "aid and attendance" to refer to Pension is that many veterans or their single surviving spouses can become eligible if they have a regular need for the *aid and attendance* of a caregiver or if they are *housebound*.

Evidence of this need for care must be certified by VA as a "rating." With a rating, certain veterans or their surviving spouses can now qualify for Pension. Pension is also available to low income veteran households without a rating, but it is a lesser dollar amount.

SUMMARY OF VA PENSION RATES

Veteran / One Dependent	Monthly	Annual
Basic Pension	1,291	15,493
Housebound	1,510	18,120
Aid and Attendance	1,949	23,396
Each additional dependent child	168	2,020
Medical deduction	64	775

Single Veteran	Monthly	Annual
Basic Pension	985	11,830
Housebound	1,204	14,457
Aid and Attendance	1,644	19,736
Each additional dependent child	168	2,020
Medical deduction	49	592

Widow	Monthly	Annual
Basic Pension	661	7,932
Housebound	808	9,696
Aid and Attendance	1,056	12,672
Each additional dependent child	168	2,020
Medical deduction	33	397

HOW COMPENSATION AND PENSION WORK TOGETHER

Compensation and Pension claims are submitted on the same form and VA will consider paying either benefit. If a claimant is awarded both benefits, the claimant can only receive one of them — typically the higher of the two. Generally, for applications associated with the cost of home care, assisted living or nursing home care, the Pension benefit results in more income. Each particular case must be looked at closely to see which is best, taking into account the long term needs of the recipient.

DEATH BENEFITS

There are also several death benefit variations of the two disability programs for single surviving spouses or dependent minor children or adult dependent children. The death benefits are beyond the scope of this book, and thus not discussed in any depth.

TWO TYPES OF PENSION CLAIMS

Although VA does not differentiate between various Pension applicants, there are, in practice, two kinds of Pension applications. The first type of application or claim as it's called by VA, deals with veteran households that do not generally require the rating mentioned above in order to receive a benefit or, as VA calls it, an award. These applicants will have household income less than the monthly allowable Pension rate. In addition, they will have very little in savings or investments. And, with no ratings, the size of their Pension awards will be much smaller.

It is my opinion that most veterans or their surviving spouses receiving Pension are in this category. I believe this is true for several reasons. One reason is that Veterans Service Representatives in the local VA regional offices who deal with the public will tell callers that Pension is only available to veteran households with low income. These VSRs tum away many potentially eligible applicants. This is probably because these VA employees are not trained sufficiently to understand the special case of veterans with higher income and high medical costs.

A second reason is that callers having significant savings or investments will be told they do not qualify as well. It is possible to rearrange your financial affairs in order to qualify for Pension. Naturally, Veterans Service Representatives will not mention this as an option. We will discuss this option in more detail later on.

A third reason is that veterans with higher income and significant assets generally don't know they can qualify for Pension under certain conditions with proper planning. No one has ever told them. As a result, they never apply.

An important fourth reason is that most people don't know that the aid and attendance Pension benefit can help cover home care costs paid to *any* person or to professional providers. As a result, most people wait much too long and don't apply until they are widowed or single, and enter a nursing home. VA then refuses to pay the benefit if the single claimant is also eligible for Medicaid.

For all these reasons, only about 28 percent of eligible veteran households actually apply for and receive Pension. It also appears that, even for those households where Pension naturally fits, VA is not doing a good job of educating potential beneficiaries about this benefit.

PENSION FOR VETERANS WHO REQUIRE A RATING

This is the second type of VA application. Claimants in this category often have income above the maximum Pension rate and they may also have significant savings or investments. Typically, this category of application requires a potential beneficiary to be paying for ongoing and expensive long term care or other medical costs.

For veteran households receiving expensive long term care services and whose incomes exceed maximum Pension rates, a rating is usually necessary in order to receive a benefit. In most cases, without a rating, there is no benefit.

Receipt of a Pension benefit in these situations is generally dependent upon whether the veteran household has a need for long term care services. But, based on the incidence of long term care in an older population, at least 60% to 80% of this group might have a good chance of qualifying for Pension at some time during their later years.

2
WHO IS ELIGIBLE FOR THE PENSION BENEFIT?

Filing a claim for long term care Pension benefits can be a time-consuming, frustrating and complicated process. It's important to get help. In my opinion, no one should ever try to do it alone. Time after time, I have seen claims rejected or delayed for many months, sometimes for years, because of seemingly trivial errors or omissions of information.

Fortunately, there is help available at no cost. But you first need to determine the type of help you need, based on your particular situation. The remainder of this book will give you all the information you need to make an informed decision.

Applications for Pension that involve a rating, require evidence of prospective, recurring medical expenses, or appointments for VA powers of attorney and fiduciaries should not be attempted without the help of VA-accredited assistance.

Applications that also involve reallocations of assets or plans to bring your income within VA limits in order to qualify should not be attempted without the help of a qualified veterans' aid and attendance lawyer. Otherwise, you may have your claim rejected or delayed by many months, or do irreparable damage to your access to Medicaid or other need-based government programs should you require a nursing home later on.

To receive Pension, a veteran must have served on active duty at least 90 days and at least one of those days had to be during a period of war. Training periods do not count toward the 90 days of service. The one day of wartime service does not mean that the veteran must have served in battle or a war zone.

The following table includes the relevant war periods

Period of War	War Periods
World War Two	December 7, 1941, through December 31, 1946.
Korean Conflict	June 27, 1950, through January 31, 1955.
Vietnam Era	August 5, 1964, through May 7, 1975. For veterans who served "in country" before August 5, 1964, the war period is February 28, 1961, through May 7, 1975.
Gulf War	August 2, 1990, through the present. Thus, the "war on terror" is considered a war period.

The veteran's discharge must be better than dishonorable.

Single surviving spouses of such veterans are also eligible. Remarriage voids the surviving spouse's right to the benefit.

If younger than 65, the veteran must be totally disabled. If age 65 and older, there is no requirement for disability. In other words, the veteran is deemed to be 100 percent disabled. There is no disability requirement for a single surviving spouse.

The veteran household cannot have income, adjusted for out-of-pocket medical expenses, exceeding the so-called "Maximum Allowable Pension Rate" (MAPR) for that veteran's Pension income category. If the adjusted income *exceeds* the MAPR, there will be no benefit.

If adjusted income is *less* than the MAPR, the veteran can receive a Pension income that is equal to the difference between the

MAPR and household income adjusted for out-of-pocket medical expenses.

The Pension benefit is calculated based on 12 months of future (projected) household income, but is paid monthly.

3
UNDERSTANDING HOW BENEFITS ARE DETERMINED

THE INCOME TEST FOR PENSION ELIGIBILITY

A special provision for calculating the Pension cash benefit allows household income to be reduced by 12 months' worth of future, unreimbursed and recurring medical expenses.

These allowable, annualized medical expenses are such things as insurance premiums, the cost of home care, the cost of paying any person to provide care, the cost of adult day care, the cost of assisted living and the cost of a nursing home facility.

In most cases, only the medical portion of these expenses is deductible unless there is a rating or unless the non-veteran spouse of a living veteran has a medical need. The rules are very complex as to what counts as medical and what doesn't.

With a rating or with a medical need for the non-veteran spouse of a living veteran, all costs associated with long term care are deductible, including such expenses as room and board for assisted living and non-medical services for home care.

This special provision can allow veteran households earning more than the annual MAPR to qualify for Pension. For example, a veteran household earning $6,000 a month could still qualify for Pension if the veteran is paying $4,500 to $6,000 or more a month for nursing home costs. The applicant must submit appropriate evidence for a rating or for a medical need and for recurring costs in order to qualify for this special provision.

VA normally does not tell applicants about this special treatment of medical expenses or how to qualify for it. This is why so many veteran households are being turned down for benefits even though they could qualify after taking appropriate steps.

DEALING WITH ASSETS THAT MAY DISQUALIFY THE VETERAN

There is also an asset test to qualify for Pension. Any asset or investment that could be easily converted into income might disqualify the claimant.

An asset ceiling of $80,000 is often cited in the media as being the test. The $80,000 has to do with VA internal filing requirements and is not an actual test, however.

In reality, there is no dollar amount for the test and any level of assets, however small, could block the award. The asset test ultimately becomes a subjective decision made by the veterans' service representative who is processing the application. As a general rule, the older the veteran, the lower the asset threshold will be because the veteran's life expectancy is less.

Some assets can be excluded for purposes of the asset test. A home used as a residence, vehicles and difficult-to-sell property are generally excluded.

Also, VA will allow assets to be transferred or converted to a stream of income in order to meet the asset test. There is no look back penalty for transferring assets as there is with Medicaid.

There are complex rules governing transfers of assets and what distinguishes income from assets. For example, certain types of retirement plans may be characterized as an asset or a stream of income, depending on the features of the particular plan.

I recommend always using a qualified aid and attendance benefit lawyer when considering the transfer of assets that may otherwise be disqualifying. It is extremely important that assets that might be gifted or converted to income also meet Medicaid gifting rules in case the veteran or the surviving spouse may have to apply for Medicaid at some future date. The attorney can help avoid Medicaid penalties associated with reallocating assets. .

> WARNING
>
> A thorough knowledge of the Medicaid asset transfer penalty rules is essential when considering whether to transfer assets to meet the VA Pension qualification rules. Otherwise irreparable damage could be done to your chances for Medicaid qualification should you require nursing home care.

THE RATING

A rating of either "aid and attendance" or "housebound" allows VA to pay additional benefits beyond the regular basic Pension benefit to help cover the additional costs associated with the added disabilities such a rating implies. A rating for these allowances is determined by a veteran service representative who has been trained to recognize from medical reports and interviews whether the veteran or his surviving spouse needs the additional care.

Determinations of a need for aid and attendance or housebound benefits may be based on medical reports and findings by private physicians or from hospital facilities. Authorization of aid and attendance benefits without a rating decision is automatic if evidence establishes the claimant is a patient in a nursing home. Aid and attendance is also automatic if the claimant is blind or nearly blind or having severe visual problems.

According to Federal regulations, the following criteria are used to determine the need for aid and attendance:

- INABILITY OF THE CLAIMANT TO DRESS OR UNDRESS HIMSELF OR HER-SELF, OR TO KEEP HIMSELF ORDINARILY CLEAN AND PRESENTABLE;
- A FREQUENT NEED OF ADJUSTMENT OF ANY SPECIAL PROSTHETIC OR ORTHOPEDIC APPLIANCES WHICH BY REASON OF THE PARTICULAR DIS-ABILITY CANNOT BE DONE WITHOUT AID; THIS WILL NOT INCLUDE THE ADJUSTMENT OF APPLIANCES WHICH NORMAL PERSONS WOULD BE UNABLE TO ADJUST WITHOUT AID, SUCH AS SUPPORTS, BELTS, LACING AT THE BACK, ETC.;
- INABILITY OF THE CLAIMANT TO FEED HIMSELF THROUGH LOSS OF COORDINATION OF UPPER EXTREMITIES OR THROUGH EXTREME WEAKNESS;
- INABILITY TO ATTEND TO THE WANTS OF NATURE; OR
- INCAPACITY, PHYSICAL OR MENTAL, WHICH REQUIRES CARE OR ASSIS-TANCE ON A REGULAR BASIS TO PROTECT THE CLAIMANT FROM HAZ-ARDS OR DANGERS INCIDENT TO HIS OR HER DAILY ENVIRONMENT.

Not all of the disabling conditions in the list above are required to exist before a favorable rating may be made. The personal functions which the veteran is unable to perform are considered in connection with his or her condition as a whole. It's only necessary that the evidence establish that the veteran is so helpless as to need "regular" (scheduled and ongoing) aid and attendance from someone else, not that there be a 24-hour need.

"Bedridden" is a definition that allows a rating for aid and attendance by itself. "Bedridden" is a condition which requires that the claimant remain in bed. A person who has voluntarily taken to bed or who has been told by the doctor to remain in bed will not necessarily receive the favorable rating for aid and attendance. There must be an actual need for personal assistance from others.

Housebound means "permanently housebound by reason of disability or disabilities." This requirement is met when the veteran or his or her widow is substantially confined to his or her dwelling and the immediate premises or, if institutionalized, to the ward or clinical area and it is reasonably certain that the disability and resultant confinement will continue throughout life.

A person who can't leave his immediate premises unless under the supervision of another person is considered housebound. This might include the inability to drive because of the disability. A housebound rating doesn't mean a person needs to be confined to a personal residence. It can apply to any place where the person is living whether in a facility or in the home of someone else.

In order to receive one of these ratings the claimant must check the "Yes" box on VA Form 21-526 (claim for a living veteran) or VA Form 21-534 (claim for death Pension for a surviving spouse) that states: "Are you claiming a special monthly Pension because you need the regular assistance of another person, are blind, nearly blind, or having severe visual problems, or are housebound?" Failure to check this box may result in no rating and in some cases a denial of the claim as well as a loss of the rating allowance.

Medical evidence for a rating for "aid and attendance" or "housebound" for living arrangements other than a nursing home should be submitted with the application to avoid a delay in the approval process. Waiting for the regional office to order medical records is a time-consuming process, mainly because doctors' offices don't respond quickly or adequately to these kinds of requests.

I recommend a report completed by the physician, and obtained by the family prior to submission of the claim. This report is then included with the initial application. Your benefits professional can provide an unofficial form "Statement of Attending Physician," which can be used to determine a rating for aid and attendance or housebound. This document should be similar to the form used internally by VA to obtain information from veterans' medical facilities for determining a rating. It should be in this format so that a veterans' service representative will recognize the information.

Ratings are requested by checking the appropriate box for aid and attendance or housebound on VA Form 21-526 or VA Form 21534 (application for the single surviving spouse of a veteran).

The non-veteran spouse of a living veteran cannot qualify for a rating and therefore may have to forgo the deduction of nonmedical expenses. However, certain medical conditions will allow long term care costs for this spouse to be deducted. You need to talk to your adviser about how to meet this requirement.

HOW PENSION IS CALCULATED

The monthly award is based on VA totaling 12 months of estimated future income and subtracting from that 12 months of estimated future, recurring and predictable medical expenses.

Allowable medical expenses are also reduced by a deductible to produce an adjusted medical expense which in turn is subtracted from the estimated 12 months of future income.

The new income derived from subtracting adjusted medical expenses from income is called "countable" income, and is known by its acronym IVAP (Income for Veterans Affairs Purposes). This countable income is then subtracted from the Maximum Allowable Pension Rate (MAPR) and that result is divided by 12 to determine the monthly income Pension award. This award is paid in addition to the family income that already exists. See the examples below.

After a Pension award, you should double check VA's calculations to make sure that no errors have been made. Such errors are quite common, and need to be corrected as quickly as possible.

Example 1: Veteran is in assisted living with aid and attendance allowance. Monthly family income is $4,000 a month. The veteran's spouse is living at home. Unreimbursed medical expenses include prescription drugs, Medicare premiums, Medicare supplement premiums, and 12 months of prospective assisted living monthly costs. Assume that the family meets the asset test.

Total 12-month future, family income from all sources	$48,000
Less future unreimbursed medical expenses adjusted for 5% of MAVP	$39,600
Total countable income or IVAP	$8,400
Couples MAVP with aid and attendance allowance	$23,396
Less countable income	$8,400
Yearly pension calculation	$14,996
Monthly pension award (yearly divided by 12)	$1,249

Example 2: Veteran receiving paid home care with aid and attendance allowance. Monthly family income is $1,900 a month. Unreimbursed medical expenses include prescription drugs, Medicare premiums, Medicare supplement premiums, and 12 months of prospective home health aide monthly costs. Assume that the family meets the asset test.

Total 12-month future, family income from all sources	$22,800
Less future unreimbursed medical expenses adjusted for 5% of MAVP	$23,760
Total countable income or IVAP	-$960
Couples MAVP with aid and attendance allowance	$23,396
Less countable income	$0
Yearly pension calculation	$23,396
Monthly pension award (yearly divided by 12)	$1,949

Example 3: Surviving spouse receiving paid home care with aid and attendance allowance. Monthly income is $850 a month. Unreimbursed medical expenses include prescription drugs, Medicare premiums, Medicare supplement premiums, and 12 months of prospective home health aide monthly costs. Assume that the surviving spouse meets the asset test.

Total 12-month future, family income from all sources	$10,200
Less future unreimbursed medical expenses adjusted for 5% of MAVP	$12,000
Total countable income or IVAP	-$1,800
Couples MAVP with aid and attendance allowance	$12,681
Less countable income	$0
Yearly pension calculation	$12,681
Monthly pension award (yearly divided by 12)	$1,056

4
USING AID AND ATTENDANCE TO PAY ANYONE FOR HOME CARE

Most people who have heard about Pension know that it will cover the costs of assisted living and, in some cases, cover nursing home costs as well But the majority of those receiving long term care in this country are in their homes. Estimates are that approximately 70% to 80% of all long term care is being provided in the home.

All of the information available about Pension overlooks the fact that this benefit can be used to pay for home care, often keeping veterans out of assisted living or a nursing home. Perhaps if more people knew this fact, more people would be applying for the benefit.

It also comes as a surprise to most people that VA will allow veterans' households to deduct the annual cost of paying any person such as family members, friends or hired help for care when determining eligibility for the Pension benefit. This annual cost is also then used to calculate the benefit based on a revised "countable income" and allows families earning more than the pension benefit to receive a Pension income from VA.

This extra income can be a welcome benefit for families struggling to provide care for loved ones at home. Under the right circumstances, this annualized medical expense for the cost of help from family members, friends or any other person providing care could create an additional household income of up to $1,056 a month for a single surviving spouse of a veteran, up to $1,644 a month for a single veteran, or up to $1,949 a month for a couple. This amount can make a huge difference in the quality of the veteran household's life.

If the disabled care recipient has been rated "housebound" or in need of "aid and attendance" by VA, all fees paid to an in-home attendant will be allowed as long as the attendant provides some medical or nursing services for the disabled person. The attendant does not have to be a licensed health professional.

Services of licensed home care providers can be deducted without any need for a rating but the pension award is a lesser amount in such cases. Services of non-licensed providers can also be deducted without a rating if there is a demonstrated special medical need.

A non-licensed in-home attendant could be just about anyone receiving pay for providing services. This might be members of the family, friends, or someone hired to live in the home.

Examples of medical or nursing services include help with activities of daily living such as dressing, bathing, toileting, ambulating, feeding, and so on. Other services might include medication reminders or supervision necessary to provide a protective environment for the care recipient in the case of dementia or Alzheimer's.

All reasonable fees paid to the individual for personal care of the disabled person and maintenance of the disabled person's immediate environment may be allowed. This includes such services as cooking and housecleaning. It isn't necessary to distinguish between "medical" and "nonmedical" services.

Services which are beyond the scope of personal care of the disabled person and maintenance of the disabled person's immediate environment may not be allowed. This might include paying the bills, providing transportation for other family members, cooking and cleaning for other family members, providing entertainment, providing transportation for personal needs other than medical, and so on.

For a disabled person who has been rated or for the non-veteran spouse of a living veteran who can show a medical need, a family member may be considered an in-home attendant, but that family member has to be paid for services duly rendered.

There is potential for fraud here where a family member may move into the home and ostensibly receive payment as a caregiver but not actually provide the level of care paid for. Documentation for this care must be provided to VA, and it is reasonable for VA to question whether the services being purchased from a family member living in the household are legitimate. Such arrangements should be extensively documented and completely arm's-length.

The care arrangements and payment must be made prior to application and there must be evidence that this care is needed on an ongoing and regular basis. I recommend that there always be a formal, written care contract and weekly invoice billing for services. Money must exchange hands and there must be evidence of this.

All of this documentation must be provided as proof to VA when making application for the pension benefit. Costs for these services must be unreimbursed, meaning these costs are not paid by insurance, by contributions from the family, or from other sources.

This is not a do-it-yourself project and requires the help of a lawyer to avoid a denial of the claim.

Let's look at the following example.

Mara, who is a divorced mother of two teenagers, moves in with her mother. Mara's mother, Lucy, has recently had a stroke and needs supervision and help.

In order to take care of her mother, Mara cannot maintain full employment outside of the home. She has found a company that will let her work at home on her computer but it isn't full time employment and it doesn't pay well.

Mara has expenses she needs to cover for existing debts and also needs to support her two teenage children. She does not have housing costs but does consume additional food, utilities, and other resources due to her presence and the presence of her children in the home. She also incurs costs related to her car such as running errands, shopping for the household, taking Lucy to doctors' appointments, and transporting her children.

Lucy's household income is $1,400 a month which consists of Social Security and a small company pension. She has about $20,000 in savings in the bank. She owns her home and a car. Mara's and Lucy's combined income is just not enough to make ends meet for both families.

Lucy is the single surviving widow of a Korean War veteran. Mara has heard of a veterans benefit lawyer who helps families in this predicament obtain the VA Pension benefit.

Michelle meets with the lawyer, who suggests that Mara and her mother enter into a contract for care in accordance with VA requirements and that Lucy pay Mara $1,300 a month to provide care. The lawyer then suggests submitting a claim for a Death Pension for Lucy.

The lawyer prepares an arm's-length agreement with all VA rules taken into account and provides Mara and Lucy with guidelines so that the care services and payments to Michelle are accurately documented.

In order for these payments to Michelle to count towards a Pension award, Lucy must have a rating from the VA for "aid and attendance" or "housebound."

The lawyer provides guidance and advice to Mara and her mother as to the VA application process. He makes sure that all of the required documentation is in place before the application is submitted. He reviews all documentation and the completed VA forms and other documentation, which Mara and her mother have filled out before final submission.

If VA allows annualization of the cost of the care contract in calculating the Pension benefit, Mara's mother should receive an award. In calculating Pension, Mara's $1,300 a month contract payment should be annualized and subtracted from her annual income. An additional medical deduction is included for Lucy's $200 a month payments for Medicare Part B, Medicare Part D, and a Medicare supplement policy.

This additional amount should be annualized and also subtracted from Lucy's income. Both the contract payments and the insurance premiums are adjusted for 5 percent of MAPR before being subtracted from Lucy's income. Her new "countable" income will be negative and subtracting that new income from the MAPR will allow Lucy to receive the maximum Pension benefit for her rating category.

After five months, VA awards Lucy $1,056 a month in additional Pension income. Her total income is now $2,456 a month. VA also awards a total of four months of benefits, payable retroactively to the first day of the month following the month in which the application was received in the regional office.

TIP

Do not delay filing your claim. A Pension award is prospective only, effective on the first day of the month following the month in which the application was received in the regional office. Filing in the wrong place or a lost application has cost veteran families many months of benefits in numerous cases.

Depending on household income and the amount of the care contract and the amount of VA Pension income, these types of care arrangements could be a welcome addition for families struggling to provide care for their loved ones at home.

Family care providers, on contract with their loved ones, do not have to be residing in the home. Caution should be exercised that these are indeed legitimate contracts and care provider arrangements and there are no behind-the-scenes transfers of monies.

5
USING AID AND ATTENDANCE TO PAY FOR PROFESSIONAL HOME CARE

Applications for Pension that involve a rating, evidence of prospective, recurring medical expenses, appointments for VA powers of attorney and fiduciaries, and the actual application process should not be attempted without professional help. I recommend that you use a VA-accredited lawyer to avoid lengthy delays in a decision or possible denials of your claim. Not only will the lawyer help you understand how to shorten the decision process from VA and ensure a successful claim but the support forms he or she provides also help you present medical evidence and costs in a format familiar to VA service representatives.

Applications that also involve reallocation of assets in order to qualify should not be attempted without the help of a qualified veterans' aid and attendance lawyer.

ANNUALIZATION OF HOME CARE COSTS

Medical expenses for home care aides are allowed prospectively for annualization if those expenses are reasonably predictable. The evidence must also show that the need for care is ongoing and regular. Expenses may be allowed whether the care recipient has a rating for aid and attendance or housebound or is not rated. However, deductible payments to a non-rated beneficiary are more restrictive.

Evidence must be submitted indicating an ongoing need for the care and the level of care in order for the Veterans Service Representative to consider the medical expense as recurring and eligible to be annualized.

Your lawyer will be able to furnish an unofficial Care Provider Report to provide evidence of recurring medical expenses in a form that can be used for this purpose. Also a copy of a written contract between the provider and the recipient, covering at least a year, and outlining the provisions and the cost should be submitted to prove the intent of the care recipient and the provider.

TIP

If the care recipient is unable to sign the care provider's contract due to infirmity or incapacity, the contract should be signed by a person legally authorized to sign on the recipient's behalf. Typically, legal authority must be delegated to an agent or attorney-in-fact under a power of attorney, to a trustee under a living trust, or under some other legally binding authority.

The non-veteran spouse of a living veteran may also be eligible for annualization of home health aide costs. If the home care is being furnished by a licensed health professional, then not much further proof is necessary other than the documentation proving the care is being provided.

If the provider is not licensed, then a medical need must be established in order to deduct these costs, in accordance with VA's expectations.

HOME CARE RECIPIENT IS NOT RATED

Payments for care at home for a recipient who is not rated for housebound or aid and attendance are only counted for annualization if made to a licensed health professional. There is an exception to this if a medical need can be established.

The term "licensed health professional" refers to an individual licensed to furnish health services by the state in which the services are provided. The term includes registered nurses, licensed vocational nurses, CNAs and licensed practical nurses. Some states also license non-medical home care providers to provide services as well. VA will also recognize these providers. Check with your lawyer to determine whether the care provider you have selected is considered licensed according to your state's rules.

All reasonable fees paid to the licensed health professional for personal care of the disabled person and maintenance of the disabled person's immediate environment may be allowed. This includes such services as cooking and housecleaning for the disabled person. It isn't necessary to distinguish between "medical" and "nonmedical" services.

Services which are beyond the scope of personal care of the disabled person and maintenance of the disabled person's immediate environment, however, may not be allowed. So, be sure to consider the list of services you want item by item.

Services beyond the scope might include services such as driving the veteran's spouse to appointments, paying bills, answering the phone, providing shopping errands for the household, and so on.

If an hourly rate is being paid to the home care provider, a portion of this rate may be disallowed for services beyond the scope of personal care.

CAUTION

Disallowance of a portion of such service costs can have a double adverse impact. First, it can reduce the amount of the monthly Pension awarded. Even more important is that it can result in the veteran's income being too high, causing complete ineligibility for the benefit. This is why careful advance planning is required in cases involving care contracts.

CARE RECIPIENT IS RATED

If the disabled care recipient has been rated "housebound" or in need of "aid and attendance" by VA, all fees paid to an in-home attendant will be allowed as long as the attendant provides some medical or nursing services for the disabled person. The attendant does not have to be a licensed health professional.

All reasonable fees paid to the individual for personal care of the disabled person and maintenance of the disabled person's immediate environment may be allowed. This includes such services as cooking and housecleaning for the disabled person. It isn't necessary to distinguish between "medical" and "nonmedical" services. As with an unrated beneficiary, however, services which are beyond the scope of personal care of the disabled person and maintenance of the disabled person's immediate environment may not be allowed.

DOCUMENTATION OF HOME CARE EXPENSES

If the fees for an in-home attendant are an allowable expense, receipts or other documentation of this expense are required.

Documentation includes any of the following:

- A RECEIPT,
- A STATEMENT ON THE PROVIDER'S LETTERHEAD,
- A COMPUTER SUMMARY,
- A LEDGER OR
- BANK STATEMENT.

The evidence submitted must include:

- THE AMOUNT PAID,
- THE DATE PAYMENT WAS MADE,
- THE PURPOSE OF THE PAYMENT (THE NATURE OF THE PRODUCT OR SERVICE PROVIDED),
- THE NAME OF THE PERSON TO OR FOR WHOM THE PRODUCT OR SERVICE WAS PROVIDED AND
- IDENTIFICATION OF THE PROVIDER TO WHOM PAYMENT WAS MADE.

6
USING AID AND ATTENDANCE TO PAY FOR ASSISTED LIVING

Applications for Pension that involve a rating, evidence of prospective, recurring medical expenses, appointments for VA powers of attorney and fiduciaries, and an understanding of the actual application process should not be attempted without professional help. I recommend that you use a VA-accredited lawyer to avoid lengthy delays in a decision or possible denials of your claim. Not only will the lawyer help you understand how to shorten the decision process from VA and ensure a successful claim but the support forms he or she provides also help you present medical evidence and costs in a format familiar to VA service representatives.

Applications that also involve reallocation of assets to qualify should not be attempted without the help of a qualified veterans aid and attendance attorney.

Assisted living, residential care, adult day care or other similar arrangements aren't categorized by VA as nursing homes. As such, annualization of costs and a rating aren't automatic. If the beneficiary isn't rated or a medical need hasn't been established, the service representative will only allow recurring unreimbursed medical expenses for specific medical care provided by licensed health professionals. Costs for room and board or custodial care can't be applied.

On the other hand, if a beneficiary residing in one of these living arrangements has been rated as having a need for "aid and attendance" or is rated "housebound" or a medical need has been established, VA will allow all reasonable costs to be counted as prospective, annualized medical expenses as long as some of those costs are paid for medical care. The providers do not have to be licensed.

In the case of Alzheimer's, the physician's statement used for rating must state that the person needing care should be in a protective environment. Otherwise, only medical costs are covered. Applying for a rating is discussed in Chapter 3. All reasonable costs would include room and board as well as other unreimbursed billable services.

TIP

Most physicians are not knowledgeable about the need for the precise wording in the physician's statement. Your VA-accredited lawyer should be able to guide your physician in the proper wording of the statement to prevent delay or rejection of your claim.

The director of the facility must sign a statement verifying the type of care being given and the fact that the person receiving the care is expected to remain a resident in the facility. Your lawyer will be able to provide a copy of a form which can be used to provide evidence of recurring medical expenses. I highly recommend that a form of this nature be submitted with the application.

A copy of the contract for services as well as invoices and statements from the facility should also be included.

There may be a possibility in some cases of a non-veteran spouse of a living veteran receiving annualized credit for recurring costs of nonnursing home facility care. Under certain conditions, a medical need can be established to allow annualizing all medical and non-medical costs. If VA allows annualization of non-medical costs such as room and board for a spouse of a living veteran, there will be no Pension allowance for aid and attendance or housebound, and the Pension award will be much smaller.

A death claim is different because the surviving spouse can receive a rating in that case.

7
USING AID AND ATTENDANCE TO PAY FOR A NURSING HOME

THE EASIEST BUT MOST DIFFICULT APPLICATION OF ALL

For a potential beneficiary in a nursing home, the application for Pension is very straightforward. The claimant simply has to check the box on form VA 21-526 or form VA 21-534 that he or she is a patient in a nursing home and provide acceptable evidence for that. An award, including an aid and attendance allowance from VA, is almost always forthcoming without any additional requirements relating to a rating. Nursing home costs are also automatically annualized.

Unfortunately, in most cases, Pension does not work well for paying the costs of a nursing home. This is because the amount of Pension income is rarely enough to cover the difference between the cost of the nursing home and the beneficiary's income. On the other hand, Medicaid will cover this difference in cost and in most cases Medicaid is a better alternative to Pension.

Eligibility for Medicaid causes difficulty for those beneficiaries who also want to receive Pension income in a nursing home.

For a single person, VA refuses to pay the full Pension benefit if that person is eligible for Medicaid and will only pay $90 a month towards nursing home costs. For a beneficiary with a spouse at home, the combination of Pension and Medicaid may not work due to the Medicaid rules. For Georgia veterans that may mean planning for Medicaid qualification under the rules administered by the Medicaid Division of the Georgia Department of Community Health.

Finally, if assets have to be gifted in order to qualify for Pension, this could make the potential Pension beneficiary ineligible for Medicaid just at the time when Medicaid assistance is most needed.

There are, however, circumstances where Pension fits very well for a beneficiary in a nursing home. I discuss these below. As easy and simple as the Pension application for a nursing home patient is, claimants should always seek the advice of a VA-accredited lawyer who understands both Medicaid and the VA benefit. There are strategies that can be pursued to make Pension for nursing home patients work out in certain cases. But few people can solve this on their own and it requires an expert to make the combination of Medicaid and Pension successful.

TIP

Georgia's Medicaid regulations require that eligible veteran households apply for VA benefits as a requirement for Medicaid eligibility. According to those regulations, "Application for VA Compensation or VA Pension must be made by individuals who may be eligible for either benefit."

ANNUALIZATION OF NURSING HOME COSTS

If the veteran or the veteran's surviving spouse is a patient in a nursing home, VA should automatically allow 12 months' worth of nursing home costs to be applied as medical expenses. The patient will also automatically receive an aid and attendance allowance. The expenses applied are out-of-pocket costs after reimbursement.

An annualized medical expense deduction can be allowed for unreimbursed nursing home fees even if the nursing home is not licensed by the state to provide skilled or intermediate level care.

The definition of a "nursing home" for purposes of the VA medical expense deduction is not the same as the definition of nursing home for other Pension purposes. A nursing home for purposes of the medical expense deduction is any facility which provides extended term, in-patient medical care.

A responsible official of the nursing home must sign a statement that the disabled claimant is a patient (as opposed to a resident) of the nursing home. VA has a form that is used for this purpose. It is called VA Form 21-0779 — Request for Nursing Home Information in Connection with Claim for Aid and Attendance.

A copy of the contract with the facility should also be included when submitting this form. Statements and evidence of payment must also be included. Canceled checks are *not* acceptable.

Veterans in Georgia's Veterans Homes may apply their out-of-pocket costs for use of the home as a recurring prospective, medical expense deduction. Again, a statement from an official of the state home indicating the veteran is a patient, not a resident, should be submitted.

In the case of a non-veteran spouse in a nursing home, where the veteran is still alive, the VA application form 21-526 does not have a provision for disclosing the spouse receiving nursing home care. The spouse nursing home cost might be eligible for annualization of medical expenses. I recommend submitting a letter along with the certification from the nursing home that the spouse is a patient. I also suggest this letter request annualization or prospective treatment of the nursing home costs.

A veteran in a nursing home will receive a rating for aid and attendance, but the non-veteran spouse of a living veteran will not.

A death claim is different because the surviving spouse can receive a rating in that case. If VA allows annualization of nursing home costs for a non-veteran spouse of a living veteran, there will be no allowance for aid and attendance, and the Pension award will be much smaller.

RETAINING VA BENEFITS AND IMPUTED INCOME

VA will not pay anything more than $90 a month if a single veteran or single surviving spouse is eligible for Medicaid covered nursing home care. Georgia veterans' homes are exempt from this ruling and those state homes that also accept Medicaid often end up with a surplus of income for the veteran. This is because Medicaid rules are not supposed to apply the allowance for aid and attendance or housebound to the cost of the facility.

This extra $395-$657 a month allowance can be used to provide extra services or goods to the veteran. This money must be spent because, if it is allowed to accumulate, it will disqualify the beneficiary for Medicaid by pushing the allowable assets above the $2,000 Georgia Medicaid limit. Accumulations may also affect the Pension benefit as well. Some state veterans' homes report pooling this money to provide outings, special parties, fishing trips and so on for their residents.

For purposes of income, VA will not count Medicaid payments as income for someone residing in a nursing home. However, Medicaid does consider VA Pension to be income that must be applied towards the cost of care. As mentioned above, Medicaid rules exclude the allowance for aid and attendance or housebound as income.

I have heard from some state veterans' organizations that not all state Medicaid departments honor this rule and will count the allowance as income as well. Also, counting Pension income for those states like Georgia that have an income test for Medicaid may create a problem for Medicaid eligibility.

The most VA will pay to offset the cost of a nursing home is $1,949 a month for a couple, $1,644 a month for a single veteran or $1,056 a month for the single surviving spouse of a veteran.

With nursing home costs ranging from $5,000-$7,000 a month, generally the VA benefit cannot cover the difference between the veteran household's income and the nursing home cost. In most cases there is a deficit. Medicaid will cover the actual difference between the Medicaid beneficiary's income and the cost of the nursing home. Medicaid is therefore a more viable benefit in the vast majority of cases.

For the reasons outlined above, many lawyers feel that trying to dovetail Medicaid with VA payments is not a useful exercise, and for those eligible for Medicaid, applying for Pension might be a waste of time. But there are situations where Medicaid may be available, and the Pension could be a valuable benefit as well. I offer an example of this further on in this book where a veteran, going through spend down to qualify for Medicaid, can receive more income that might be used for the spouse living at home.

In appropriate cases, Pension income can be used to lengthen the spend down process, and if the veteran dies while going through this process, valuable assets have been retained for the benefit of the veteran's family. These assets can make a significant difference in the quality of life for the surviving spouse.

Another use for the Pension benefit associated with nursing home care is when the single veteran or surviving spouse might be eligible for Medicaid, but there is a statewide waiting list for Medicaid beds. With the expected shrinking of both federal and state government budgets, this situation is more likely to occur in the future. The Pension benefit allows the veteran, the surviving spouse, or his or her family additional money to cover part of the cost of private pay until a Medicaid bed becomes available.

For the beneficiary who is eligible for Medicaid and has dependents at home, sharing the Pension with Medicaid may be more useful than allowing Medicaid to pay the entire bill. Some state Medicaid programs encourage veterans with dependents to apply for Pension because it reduces Medicaid's liability for the cost. Other states, like Georgia, require it.

In certain situations, the VA benefit available to a married veteran with an aid and attendance allowance can save money overall. Residency in a nursing home automatically includes the VA aid and attendance allowance. With some planning, it is possible for Medicaid and VA Pension could work together in providing more income for a veteran household or preserve savings of the spouse that's not in the nursing home.

As a general rule, VA Pension doesn't work well with Medicaid unless there is a spend down period or the nursing home has no Medicaid beds. If Medicaid is available immediately it is unlikely that VA Pension would be needed.

TIP

I strongly recommend in such cases that you contact a VA-accredited lawyer who is proficient in both planning for VA benefits and in Medicaid planning. To try and understand what the best solution is by yourself is probably not possible without a thorough knowledge of both the Medicaid and Pension laws and regulations.

Whether the combination of the two benefits or Medicaid alone is better must be considered case-by-case, requiring financial projections be done by someone familiar with the Medicaid and VA rules. Such things to consider are the spousal minimum monthly income allowed by Medicaid and whether Medicaid's payments on behalf of John will become part of an "estate recovery" effort by the state after the nursing home resident dies. Georgia has expanded, comprehensive estate recovery regulations that would have to be taken into account when planning to use both VA and Medicaid benefits.

8
UNDERSTANDING THE APPLICATION PROCESS FOR PENSION

UNDERSTANDING HOW PENSION FITS IN AT VA

Pension (aid and attendance benefit) and its associated benefit, Compensation, are the two principal disability income programs available to veterans. Compensation is the more heavily used benefit and is available to veterans who have service-connected disabilities. VA estimates about 35 percent of all currently discharging veterans will apply for Compensation some time during their lives.

Pension is a lesser used benefit and a lesser known disability income that is available to veterans who served during a period of war. Pension is available to wartime veterans who are non-service-connected disabled or age 65 and older.

Special death benefit arrangements related to these two disability programs are also available to surviving dependents of veterans.

Claims for Compensation and Pension are submitted on the same application form and VA can grant either one. Generally, Compensation is the more desirable benefit because there is no income or asset test and it's not taxable as income.

Pension works best for veteran households with low income who do not qualify for Compensation. Pension also fits well for veteran households with higher incomes and high costs of long term care services. In these cases, Pension may be a better alternative to Compensation.

THE DEPARTMENT OF VETERANS AFFAIRS

The Department of Veterans Affairs is the second largest federal agency, employing over 218,000 full-time workers. The Secretary of Veterans Affairs is a member of the President's Cabinet.

VA is divided into three benefit divisions:

- VETERANS HEALTH ADMINISTRATION (VHA)
- VETERANS BENEFITS ADMINISTRATION (VBA)
- NATIONAL CEMETERY ADMINISTRATION (NCA)

There are also numerous other administrative and support divisions in the Department of Veterans Affairs devoted to supporting the various benefit programs available to veterans. These benefit programs are:

National Cemetery Administration It oversees cemeteries for veterans and the grave marker program.

Veterans Health Administration. It provides comprehensive medical care which also includes prescription drugs, long-term care services, counseling, prosthetics and orthotics, hearing clinics, vision clinics and limited dental services and eyeglasses for a select number of veterans.

Not all veterans can get into the health care system because or funding limitations, and Veterans Health is now limited to income means-tested veterans and veterans with service connected disabilities. Veterans' health care has in recent years been cited by the media as being the best health care service in America, based on treatment outcome and patient satisfaction.

Veterans Benefits Administration. It manages the Compensation and Pension programs, tuition assistance for veterans and reservists, vocational rehabilitation and employment services,

VA-guaranteed housing loans and stipends for certain veterans for burial and grave markers. VBA also administers six life insurance plans for certain veteran, reservist and active-duty service groups and oversees two additional life insurance plans administered by Prudential Insurance Company.

The Veterans Benefits Administration manages its benefit programs through 57 regional offices located in 49 states (Wyoming is not included), the District of Columbia, Puerto Rico and the Philippines . Each state, except Wyoming, has a least one regional office. California has three ROs and Texas, Pennsylvania and New York each have two offices.

Compensation, Pension and burial benefits are managed out of each of the 57 offices for the territory in which the office is located. With the exceptions of the larger states mentioned above, the territory of each regional office is the state in which it is located. States with more than one regional office serve specified geographic areas in that state. Pension Eligibility Verification Reports (EVR's) and income matching for Pension are administered in the St. Paul, Philadelphia and Milwaukee regional offices.

All Pension applications are managed through these administrative offices. Much of the annual reporting and application procedures for Pension are now on the internet for online input.

PENSION CLAIMS PROCESSING IN THE REGIONAL OFFICE

Applications for first-time Pension claims are mailed to the regional office of the state in which the claimant resides. For those states with more than one regional office, the claimant must find out which area the office serves and mail the application to the appropriate regional office.

Upon receiving an original application for claim in the office, workers will date-stamp the document and send a verification letter back to the person making application. This date becomes the effective date of the claim. If an award is granted, retroactive payments are made back to the first of the month following the month of the effective date. After making copies of and certifying the original discharge papers, these papers will also be sent back to the applicant.

VA has divided the application process into an assembly line where each function along the line has a responsibility for additional information. When a claim is fully developed for a rating decision — which is required with many Pension claims — it is sent to the Rating Team for a final decision. Finally, the claim is handed off to a post-determination team that handles final notifications, arrangements for payment, and so on.

VA's assembly line approach to the handling of claims folders results in many different VA employees handling those folders. It is an extraordinarily inefficient method of claims processing from the claimant's point of view. VA employees spend a great deal of time trying to match claimants' documents that arrive by mail with the claimant's folder.

The result is VA frequently requests documents from claimants when those documents have already been submitted, delays, and numerous other problems. So do not be surprised of your claim encounters such problems. Be patient but persistent.

THE RATING TEAM

The Rating Team's primary function is to make a determination on claims that have been developed to the point where a rating decision can be made. Veterans Service Representatives have been trained to issue ratings based on medical information from doctors' records and reports.

For Compensation claims, this expertise requires determining a level of disability such as 10 percent disabled, 30 percent disabled, and so on. The majority of Compensation claims require a determination of disability. Compensation claims may not require a rating depending on how the veteran died.

Claims for Pension require the rating function determine initial eligibility for veterans younger than 65 based on the requirement for total disability. A Rating VSR must also determine from medical information whether there is an additional need for aid and attendance or if the claimant is housebound. Finally, the rating function for Pension must determine whether the level of household assets might disqualify a claim. Not all applications for Pension require a rating.

When the term "rating" as used in conjunction with Pension, it can mean two things. Rating can mean that the claim was awarded or denied based on a decision by the Rating Team in the regional office. Rating can also mean that an additional allowance for aid and attendance or housebound was awarded. These allowances are often called "ratings" as well.

GETTING A PENSION CLAIM THROUGH THE SYSTEM FASTER

A so-called "triage" team in the regional office examines all initial claims for accuracy and completeness of information. If the claim is unsigned or if important boxes on the forms are left blank, these deficiencies are marked in red and the application form is sent back to the applicant and must be resubmitted by the claimant. If discharge papers aren't included this could slow down the process by several months. If a proper VA power of attorney has not been prepared, another few months might go by while awaiting the correct document.

Triage team members are looking for a claim that is "substantially complete." Claims that seem to have all the requirements are passed on to the Pre-Determination Team. This team determines the need for additional documentation in order to prepare the claim for a rating if a rating is necessary. If a rating is not necessary, a final decision could be made at this point.

If the claimant is accurate in filling out the form, in providing proper discharge papers and proof of relationship, and in providing the proper VA power of attorney or guardianship proof, the initial claim is well on the road to being approved more quickly.

Another important issue in submitting a well-documented claim is knowing, in advance, what evidence and documents are required for a rating decision. By providing those documents upfront and not waiting for VA to come back with a request, the claim can be passed by the triage team immediately to the rating activity for a final decision. This might cut the time for a decision by several months.

The secret to shortening the time from submission to a decision is to anticipate all of the documentation requirements that are necessary and submit them with the initial application.

The following is a list of the most commonly-required documents you will need to submit with your claim for the Aid and Attendance Pension:

- DISCHARGE/SEPARATION PAPERS (DD-214). IF YOU NEED TO REQUEST MILITARY RECORDS, YOU CAN VISIT HTTP://WWW.ARCHIVES.GOV/ST-LOUIS/MILITARY-PERSONNEL/STANDARD-FORM-180.HTML OR WWW.VA.GOV THEN LOOK FOR THE LINK FOR MILITARY RECORDS ON THE RIGHT SIDE. THIS IS A SHORT CUT TO THE ARCHIVE SITE. FULL INSTRUCTIONS ON HOW TO REQUEST MILITARY RECORDS IS LISTED ON THE LATTER SITE.
- COPY OF MARRIAGE CERTIFICATE AND ALL MARITAL INFORMATION IF BENEFIT IS BASED ON MARRIAGE.
- COPY OF BIRTH CERTIFICATE(S).
- COPY OF THE DEATH CERTIFICATE (SURVIVING SPOUSE CASES ONLY).
- COPY OF THE CURRENT SOCIAL SECURITY AWARD LETTER (THE LETTER THAT SOCIAL SECURITY SENDS AT THE BEGINNING OF THE YEAR STATING WHAT YOUR MONTHLY AMOUNT WILL BE FOR THE FOLLOWING YEAR).
- NET WORTH INFORMATION, INCLUDING BANK ACCOUNTS, CDS, TRUSTS, STOCKS, BONDS, ANNUITIES, ETC.
- PROOF OF ALL INCOME FROM PENSIONS, RETIREMENT, INTEREST INCOME FROM INVESTMENTS, ANNUITIES, ETC.
- IF YOU ARE A COURT-APPOINTED GUARDIAN OF THE VETERAN OR SURVIVING SPOUSE, A CERTIFIED COPY OF THE COURT ORDER OF THE APPOINTMENT IS REQUIRED.
- PROOF OF INSURANCE PREMIUMS, MEDICATIONS, MEDICAL BILLS OR ANY OTHER MEDICAL EXPENSES THAT ARE NOT REIMBURSED BY INSURANCE, MEDICARE, OR MEDICAID.
- PHYSICIAN STATEMENT THAT INCLUDES CURRENT DIAGNOSIS, MEDICAL STATUS, PROGNOSIS, NAME AND ADDRESS, ABILITY TO CARE FOR SELF, ABILITY TO TRAVEL UNATTENDED, ETC. IF YOU ARE A VETERAN IN A NURSING HOME, OR A FAMILY MEMBER OF A VETERAN IN A NURSING HOME,

YOUR LAWYER CAN PROVIDE A FORM THAT CAN BE USED AS A CERTIFI-CATION OF THAT STATUS.

- BANKING INFORMATION FOR DIRECT DEPOSIT OF VA PENSION MONTHLY PAYMENTS (INCLUDE A VOIDED CHECK).
- EMPLOYMENT HISTORY (DOES NOT APPLY IF YOU ARE OVER 65).
- LIST OF ALL DOCTORS AND HOSPITALS VISITED IN THE LAST YEAR.

9
SUBMITTING A CLAIM FOR THE PENSION BENEFIT

THE TWO TYPES OF PENSION CLAIMS

As mentioned in Chapter 1, there are two types of Pension applications. The first of these is the application for veteran households with low income and few assets. For living veterans under the age of 65, medical evidence must also be submitted for proof of total disability. For living veterans, age 65 and older, there is no requirement to be disabled. Single surviving spouses of veterans also have no requirement for disability. These low income applications may or may not have a need for an additional rating to receive an aid and attendance or housebound allowance.

The second type of application is one where the household may have higher income and assets but one or more members of the household are incurring the high costs of long term care. These costs may be for the following types of services:

- PAYING MEMBERS OF THE FAMILY TO PROVIDE CARE AT HOME
- PAYING PROFESSIONAL PROVIDERS TO PROVIDE CARE AT HOME
- PAYING FOR THE COST OF ADULT DAY CARE

- PAYING FOR THE COST OF ASSISTED LIVING
- PAYING FOR THE COST OF A NURSING HOME

These types of claims require appropriate medical evidence in order to receive a rating for aid and attendance or housebound allowances. In certain cases medical evidence can be produced where a rating cannot be allowed such as with the non-veteran spouse of a living veteran. This medical evidence must be received or the non-medical expenses associated with long term care are not deductible from income.

These claims require special documentation and evidence. In addition, those households with substantial assets will be ineligible for Pension income unless those assets can be eliminated from the veteran's assets. If assets appear to be disqualifying, a claimant should contact a VA-accredited lawyer who can provide advice on asset reallocation strategies.

Claims for this second type of application are the more challenging and difficult ones to process. I recommend you use a lawyer to help you with these types of claims, especially when Medicaid eligibility may be required now or in the future.

Here are the official and unofficial forms associated with submitting a Pension claim:

- VA FORM 21-526 — VETERAN'S APPLICATION FOR COMPENSATION AND/OR PENSION, PARTS A,B,C, & D
- VA FORM 21-534 — APPLICATION FOR DEPENDENCY AND INDEMNITY COMPENSATION, DEATH PENSION AND ACCRUED BENEFITS BY A SURVIVING SPOUSE OR CHILD (INCLUDING DEATH COMPENSATION IF APPLICABLE)
- SF 180 — REQUEST PERTAINING TO MILITARY RECORDS (USED TO OBTAIN DISCHARGE RECORD)
- VA FORM 21-22A — APPOINTMENT OF INDIVIDUAL AS CLAIMANT'S REPRESENTATIVE (POA FOR CLAIM)
- VA FORM 21-0779 — REQUEST FOR NURSING HOME INFORMATION IN CONNECTION WITH CLAIM FOR AID AND ATTENDANCE
- VA FORM 10-10EZ — APPLICATION FOR HEALTH BENEFITS (VETERANS RECEIVING PENSION ARE GUARANTEED HEALTH BENEFITS WITHOUT COPAYMENT)

- VA FORM 10-0103 — VETERAN'S APPLICATION FOR ASSISTANCE IN ACQUIRING HOME IMPROVEMENT AND STRUCTURAL ALTERATIONS (HISA) (AVAILABLE TO PENSION RECIPIENTS WITH RATINGS)
- STATEMENT OF ATTENDING PHYSICIAN (USED TO DETERMINE RATING FOR AID AND ATTENDANCE OR HOUSEBOUND) THERE IS NOT AN OFFICIAL VA FORM FOR THIS. SEE YOUR LAWYER.
- CARE PROVIDER REPORT (USED TO PROVIDE EVIDENCE OF RECURRING MEDICAL EXPENSES) THERE IS NOT AN OFFICIAL VA FORM FOR THIS. SEE YOUR LAWYER.
- HEALTH INSURANCE PREMIUMS (USED TO PROVIDE EVIDENCE OF RECURRING MEDICAL EXPENSES) THERE IS NOT AN OFFICIAL VA FORM FOR THIS. SEE YOUR LAWYER.
- CLAIMANT'S CERTIFICATION (VERIFIES OUT-OF-POCKET COSTS FOR UNREIMBURSED MEDICAL EXPENSES) THERE IS NOT AN OFFICIAL VA FORM FOR THIS. SEE YOUR LAWYER.

10
DEATH CLAIMS AND SPECIAL BENEFITS

DEATH BENEFITS AVAILABLE USING VA FORMS 21-534 AND 21-530

Death benefits are available for a single surviving spouse of a veteran or for a dependent child of a veteran or for parents of a veteran who died during wartime. The following benefits are available for surviving spouses and dependent children:

- DEPENDENCY AND INDEMNITY COMPENSATION (DIC),
- DEATH PENSION,
- ACCRUED BENEFITS AND
- BURIAL AND MEMORIAL BENEFITS.

DIC, death pension and accrued benefits are claimed on VA Form 21-534. Burial and Memorial benefits are claimed on VA Form 21-530.

The claims process for compensation and pension is basically the same as the process for Compensation and Pension outlined in Chapter 9, using VA Form 21-526 — the form used for living veterans. The documentation and request for ratings and recurring prospective medical payments is the same as outlined in previous chapters.

ACCRUED BENEFITS

Accrued benefits are benefits that may have been payable to the veteran before his or her death. Most commonly these are benefits that were being applied for but the veteran died before a decision was made. This could be Compensation or Pension. The rule is if VA had all of the necessary paperwork in order to make a decision and a favorable decision would have been the outcome then the surviving spouse or a dependent child of the veteran is entitled to the benefit that would have been paid. If there is a larger death benefit available to the spouse, the larger of the accrued or death benefit is paid to the spouse or dependent child. The benefit is payable in the month of the veteran's death.

As an example, VA receives the veteran's application for pension or compensation on June 14, 2011, and all of the paperwork has been submitted up until September 20 when the veteran dies. The surviving spouse notifies VA of the death and immediately a VA Form 21-534 is mailed to her. She files the form and, depending on the decision from VA, she potentially has a choice of three benefits. If the decision for the deceased veteran is favorable, she may be entitled to either Compensation or Pension payable for the month of September. The surviving spouse may also be entitled to a death pension and may choose to take that if it is a larger amount.

If there is no surviving spouse or dependent child to pay an accrued benefit then VA will pay the cost of final expenses and burial to the person who had to pay these costs. These would be costs that were not reimbursed by insurance or prepaid plans.

VA sends a special form to the person who took care of the final arrangements and appropriate paperwork must be submitted to make a claim.

VA BURIAL ALLOWANCES

VA burial allowances are partial reimbursements of an eligible veteran's burial and funeral costs. When the cause of death is not service-related, the reimbursements are generally described as two payments: (1) a burial and funeral expense allowance, and (2) a plot interment allowance. You may be eligible for a VA burial allowance if:

- YOU PAID FOR A VETERAN'S BURIAL OR FUNERAL,
- YOU HAVE NOT BEEN REIMBURSED BY ANOTHER GOVERNMENT AGENCY OR SOME OTHER SOURCE, SUCH AS THE DECEASED VETERAN'S EMPLOYER AND
- THE VETERAN WAS DISCHARGED UNDER CONDITIONS OTHER THAN DISHONORABLE.

In addition, at least one of the following conditions must be met:

- THE VETERAN DIED BECAUSE OF A SERVICE-RELATED DISABILITY,
- THE VETERAN WAS RECEIVING VA PENSION OR COMPENSATION AT THE TIME OF DEATH,
- THE VETERAN WAS ENTITLED TO RECEIVE VA PENSION OR COMPENSATION, BUT DECIDED NOT TO REDUCE HIS/HER MILITARY RETIREMENT OR DISABILITY PAY, OR
- THE VETERAN DIED IN A VA HOSPITAL, IN A NURSING HOME UNDER VA CONTRACT, OR WHILE IN AN APPROVED STATE NURSING HOME.

SERVICE-RELATED DEATH

VA will pay up to $2,000 toward burial expenses for deaths on or after September 11, 2001. VA will pay up to $1,500 for deaths prior to September 10, 2001. If the veteran is buried in a VA national cemetery, some or all of the cost of transporting the deceased may be reimbursed.

NON-SERVICE-RELATED DEATH

VA will pay up to $300 toward burial and funeral expenses, and a $300 plot-interment allowance for deaths on or after December 1, 2001. The plot-interment allowance is $150 for deaths prior to December 1, 2001. If the death happened while the veteran was in a VA hospital or under VA contracted nursing home care, some or all of the costs for transporting the deceased's remains may be reimbursed.

You can apply by filling out VA Form 21-530, Application for Burial Benefits. You should attach proof of the veteran's military service (DD 214), a death certificate, and copies of funeral and burial bills you have paid.

OTHER DEATH BENEFITS

Burial in VA National Cemeteries
Headstones and markers
Presidential memorial certificates
Burial flags

HISA GRANTS

If you are interested in applying for one of these grants you should contact a VA-accredited lawyer, a financial adviser or a home care agency that is familiar with the application process.

U.S. law authorizes the Secretary of Veterans Affairs to provide Home Improvements and Structural Alterations (HISA) grants to eligible veterans. The lifetime benefit limitation for service connected HISA benefits is $4,100, and $1,200 for non-service connected HISA benefits.

The HISA benefit is limited to the improvement and structural alterations necessary only to assure the continuation of treatment and/or provide access to the home or to essential lavatory and sanitary facilities.

NOTE:

It does not include those improvements which would serve only to lend comfort to the individual or make life outside the health care facility more acceptable.

Here are the types of projects that HISA grants will pay for. This list is not all-inclusive and other appropriate projects may be approved, depending on the facts of the particular case.

1) Roll-in showers
2) Construction of wooden or concrete, permanent ramping to provide access to the home

3) Widening doorways to bedroom, bathroom, etc., to achieve wheelchair access
4) Lowering of kitchen or bathroom counters and sinks
5) Improving entrance paths and driveways in immediate area of home to facilitate access to the home
6) Construction of concrete pads and installation of exterior types of wheelchair lift mechanisms if the installation cost exceeds $500
7) Interior and exterior railing deemed necessary for patients with ambulatory capability or for veterans rated legally blind if the installation cost is over $500

11
PRACTICAL ADVICE ON THE VA AID AND ATTENDANCE PENSION APPLICATION PROCESS

This chapter is different from the previous ones. It's intended to alert you to some of the challenges and obstacles you may encounter when you prepare and submit your application for the Pension Aid and Attendance benefit.

The opinions expressed are my own, after having been through this process with many veterans and their families. It is my hope that this information will be helpful when navigating the complicated application process.

The chapter includes answers to frequently asked questions, practical tips, and insights which may make your experience less frustrating.

If you are looking for information on VA subjects that are beyond the scope of this book, go here: .

My web site: http://davisnelsonlaw.com
My blog: http://davisnelsonlaw.com/davis-blog

IS IT WORTH YOUR TIME AND EFFORT TO APPLY FOR THIS BENEFIT?

Yes! With both a veteran and the veteran's spouse in assisted living, over time, this benefit could be worth $150,000 or more in additional income to offset living expenses. For many families dealing with the escalating cost of either assisted living or nursing home care, this benefit can make a big difference in the quality of care and the residence a veteran is able to afford. It is most definitely worth the effort!

WHO SHOULD PREPARE AND SUBMIT YOUR PENSION CLAIM?

At one time there were several companies that specialized in helping you apply for this benefit. They knew how to cut through the "red tape." Their expertise in this area was invaluable, and usually resulted in the application being approved in the less than the standard time of nine months. However, due to the VA's reinterpretation of when a claim is started, these companies were forced to stop assisting claimants.

Although the VA has closed a number of businesses that were dealing with this issue, there still are individuals who have seized this demand as a "business opportunity" and offer filing services, usually in an attempt to sell the veteran annuities or other financial products. Generally, they also are poorly versed in the laws and application process of the VA, Medicaid and tax law. In addition, there are very few attorneys, CPAs or financial planners that have more than a passing knowledge of the VA Rules and Regulations. Do your homework and know who you are dealing with.

Usually, a VA-accredited lawyer is the best starting point. The lawyer should be able to quickly determine whether you are eligible or could become eligible with some planning. If your situation does not require legal assistance, the lawyer should be able to refer you to someone experienced with the claim process. *Please do not do it yourself . . . you are likely to regret it!*

THE TIME FOR FILING YOUR CLAIM IS CRITICAL!

At the present time the VA will not recognize a claim until the application is submitted. VA's regulations will not recognize a claim as being valid until the claimant has satisfied *all* of the conditions of the Pension and has submitted a statement that they wish to file a claim. A prematurely filed claim thus can cost you months of lost benefits.

Waiting to file a claim can be just as costly. Each month of delay in filing can be another month of lost benefits. Many veterans waste months trying to complete all of the required information themselves. Others wait until they are in need of nursing home care before applying because they did not realize that the benefit can be used to pay for at-home care and assisted living.

IT WILL COST YOU NOTHING TO HAVE SOMEONE PREPARE AND SUBMIT YOU CLAIM ON YOUR BEHALF, SO DON'T DO IT YOURSELF

No one is allowed to charge you a fee to assist with the filing of an initial Pension claim.

Many conscientious adult children of elderly veterans try to take on the job of submitting the claim. This is generally a waste of the child's time and a high risk strategy. In some cases, it can even be illegal. If your parent is a veteran, resist the urge to do it yourself. Turn the job over to someone knowledgeable. It will cost nothing to do so, and the finished product is likely to be superior to what you will do.

MISCELLANEOUS TRICKS AND TIPS

- IF YOU CALL OR VISIT YOUR LOCAL DEPARTMENT OF VETERANS' AFFAIRS FOR INFORMATION ON THIS BENEFIT, DO NOT BE SURPRISED IF THE INDIVIDUAL WITH WHOM YOU SPEAK DOES NOT KNOW ABOUT THIS BENEFIT OR ISN'T KNOWLEDGEABLE ABOUT IT. YOU WILL HAVE TO BE PERSISTENT IN GETTING TO SPEAK WITH SOMEONE WHO DOES. THIS IS ONE OF THE MORE COMMON COMPLAINTS I HEAR.

- THE VA MAY NOT GIVE YOU ALL OF THE REQUIRED FORMS. IT IS MY EXPERIENCE THAT THEY WILL GIVE THE CLAIMANT THE APPLICATION FORM, BUT NOT ALL OF THE OTHER FORMS THE VA WILL ASK FOR LATER. THIS IS A COMMON SOURCE OF CLAIM REJECTIONS AND DELAYS IN VETERANS RECEIVING THEIR FIRST CHECK.

- IT IS EXTREMELY IMPORTANT TO SUBMIT A COMPLETE FILE THAT WILL ANTICIPATE WHAT THE CLAIMS OFFICER WILL WANT OR NEED AND SUBMIT EVERYTHING WITH THE INITIAL APPLICATION. TO HAVE THE CLAIM APPROVED AS QUICKLY AS POSSIBLE, YOU MUST MAKE IT EASY FOR THE CLAIMS OFFICER TO COMPLETE YOUR CLAIM THE FIRST TIME THEY REVIEW IT. MAKE THEIR JOB AS EASY AS POSSIBLE.

- IF YOUR ASSETS TOTAL MORE THAN THE ALLOWABLE AMOUNT ($80,000 OR LOWER, VARYING WITH LIFE EXPECTANCY AND OTHER FACTORS), YOU NEED TO DISCUSS YOUR OPTIONS WITH A VA-ACCREDITED LAWYER WHO IS KNOWLEDGEABLE ABOUT VA BENEFITS, FINANCIAL ISSUES AND TAX LAWS IN ORDER TO REARRANGE YOUR ASSETS TO QUALIFY WITHOUT CAUSING TAX PROBLEMS.

- KEEPING THE MAXIMUM AMOUNT OF ASSETS ALLOWED BY THE VA MAY NOT BE THE BEST COURSE OF ACTION IN MANY CASES BECAUSE MEDICAID PLANNING SHOULD BE CONSIDERED IN CONJUNCTION WITH VA PLANNING. THE VA RULES AND THE MEDICAID RULES ARE VERY DIFFERENT, AND ARE IN CONFLICT IN IMPORTANT WAYS.

- THE VA MAY TELL YOU THAT YOU HAVE TOO MUCH INCOME. THEY FREQUENTLY NEGLECT TO TELL YOU THAT THE REAL INCOME NUMBER THEY NEED TO WORK FROM IS YOUR GROSS INCOME MINUS YOUR UNREIMBURSED (OUT-OF-POCKET) RECURRING MEDICAL EXPENSES. THEY TURN AWAY THE MOST CLAIMANTS WITH THIS MISTAKE, EVEN THOUGH THE CLAIMANTS ARE ELIGIBLE.

- THE APPLICATION PROCESS TAKES APPROXIMATELY NINE MONTHS (POSSIBLY LONGER) FOR YOU TO RECEIVE A "DETERMINATION OF ELIGIBILITY." YOU MUST BE PROACTIVE IN MAKING SURE THAT YOU HAVE ALL OF THE REQUIRED DOCUMENTATION WHEN YOU BEGIN YOUR APPLICATION, OR YOU WILL ENCOUNTER ADDITIONAL DELAYS.

- BE AWARE THAT IF YOU FILE YOUR CLAIM IN THE STATE WHERE YOU LIVE, BUT YOUR PARENT OR LOVED ONE IS IN A DIFFERENT STATE THAN THE ONE IN WHICH YOU FILED THE CLAIM ON THEIR BEHALF, YOU CANNOT CALL THE STATE IN WHICH THE APPLICANT RESIDES TO SPEAK WITH ANYONE ABOUT THE APPLICATION. THE INFORMATION ASSOCIATED WITH THE CLAIM IS ONLY ACCESSIBLE BY THE OFFICE IN THE STATE WHERE THE CLAIM WAS FILED.

DEMENTIA AND ALZHEIMER'S

If you or your loved one have any mental incapacities such as dementia or Alzheimer's documented by the physician who will be providing the medical letter, be aware that the VA will require that a fiduciary be appointed because the individual will be deemed incompetent for handling his or her own financial affairs.

This fact will not be brought to your attention by VA in the beginning of your application process, and could be responsible for delaying payment for any monies due to applicant for a lengthy period of time.

The application process will be put on hold as they will require that one of their representatives meet and interview the applicant in person. The process and the length of time for the VA to actually send one of their representatives for this meeting can take several months, and they will not release the funds under any circumstances until this has been done.

In addition, they will then have to assign a fiduciary of their choosing, which will increase the wait time even more.

If there is already a fiduciary in place who handles the financial affairs for the applicant, be emphatic up front to make sure they are aware of it. Ask VA to schedule an appointment for not only the applicant, but the guardian who is acting in this capacity. This could avoid imposed delays rather than being informed of their policy and procedures well into the process.

The VA will have to approve the individual who acts as the fiduciary as someone reputable to handle the financial affairs according to their guidelines.

DEATH OF THE CLAIMANT WHILE CLAIM IS PENDING

If the applicant should die prior to "approved benefits" being released, this benefit money is considered to be "accrued benefits," and you are entitled to file against these funds to help offset any and all funeral expenses that were not covered by other means such as pre-paid funeral arrangements, insurance policies, and the like.

VA may not make you aware this option is available, and you may have to go to the local office in the state in which you filed to pursue this. Once again, be persistent in speaking with someone who can assist you.

You will need to have an original copy of the death certificate, all the bills related to the cost of burial, which also includes appropriate grave markers. This process will take up to another additional six months to get it signed off and for monies to be disbursed to the individual who actually paid for the expenses.

FINAL THOUGHTS

Even though you may not have immediate need of Pension, but suspect that you might in the near future, start gathering all the necessary documents and forms well in advance so you will be prepared when the time comes.

Most adult children of veterans may not have immediate access to or knowledge of the location of discharge papers, marriage licenses, bank account information, and other important documents. In some cases, it may be necessary to arrange for copies, and this can be a timely process.

In review, you will need to be persistent and, at times, aggressive. You need to expect to encounter delays by the VA, and to be overwhelmed at times with the amount of documentation and forms that are not easy to understand.

Don't take "no" for an answer and if you encounter an individual who truly is not well informed about this benefit, keep going until you find someone who is.

It is regrettable that our government does not do more to disseminate critical information regarding benefits and pensions to those who have proudly served our country and are entitled to these by their service, so I ask that you please share this information with everyone you know who may be able to benefit.

GOD BLESS OUR VETERANS AND THEIR FAMILIES